SACRED READING

for Advent and Christmas
2018–2019

Pope's Worldwide
Prayer Network

AVE MARIA PRESS AVE Notre Dame, Indiana

Writing Team
Douglas Leonard
William Blazek, S.J.
Richard Buhler, S.J.

Scripture quotations are from *New Revised Standard Version Bible*, copyright © 1989 National Council of the Churches of Christ in the United States of America. Used by permission. All rights reserved.

© 2018 by Pope's Worldwide Prayer Network

All rights reserved. No part of this book may be used or reproduced in any manner whatsoever, except in the case of reprints in the context of reviews, without written permission from Ave Maria Press®, Inc., P.O. Box 428, Notre Dame, IN 46556, 1-800-282-1865.

Founded in 1865, Ave Maria Press is a ministry of the United States Province of Holy Cross.

www.avemariapress.com

Paperback: ISBN-13 978-1-59471-853-3

E-book: ISBN-13 978-1-59471-854-0

Cover and text design by David Scholtes.

Printed and bound in the United States of America.

CONTENTS

INTRODUCTION

It is with great joy that we introduce this 2019 edition of *Sacred Reading*. The Pope's Worldwide Prayer Network—known for so many decades as the Apostleship of Prayer—celebrates its 175th anniversary this year, with a special Papal Mass at St. Peter's Basilica on the Feast of the Most Sacred Heart of Jesus. Thanks be to God for our worldwide network! Thanks be to God for our apostleship!

Who could have anticipated that the Apostleship of Prayer, which began in 1844 in a house of formation for young Jesuits in the south of France, would grow into an international movement spanning ninety-eight countries and four continents? Those young Jesuits in Vals, France, were eager to serve in the foreign missions, yet they grew frustrated with the long, weary years of study and formation. It was at Mass on the Feast of St. Francis Xavier—December 3, 1844—that our founder, Fr. Francis Xavier Gautrelet, S.J., recounted how that great missionary had given his entire life to following Jesus Christ and that those celebrating his memory must do the same. The patron of the universal missions, St. Francis Xavier voyaged as far as the coast of China, passing through many trials and difficulties, entirely committed to service of the Lord. Fr. Gautrelet encouraged his charges to do likewise, not just in foreign lands but also in their own houses of religious formation. He suggested a way of being apostles and missionaries in daily life, uniting everything that they were doing throughout the day with Christ.

One hundred seventy-five years later, the Pope's Worldwide Prayer Network continues to address the challenges facing humanity and assist the mission of the Church. It is our vision, through prayer and work to meet the challenges of the world identified by the pope. His intentions are keys for our prayer and mission. We have a mission: we are apostles in daily life, walking a spiritual path called the "Way of the Heart" and working to serve Christ's mission. Along with the spirit of St. Francis Xavier, we rely on the spirit of our copatroness, St. Thérèse of Lisiuex, herself an Apostleship of Prayer member who desired to pray for the intentions of the Holy Father.

Friends, since 2010, the Apostleship of Prayer has been involved in a deep period of self-examination and, after prayer and reflection, recreated itself as the Pope's Worldwide Prayer Network. In 2015 we launched our new name and logo, and we released our updated digital prayer resources soon thereafter: these include our app, Click to Pray, and the monthly Pope Video, in which the Holy Father personally announces and explains his prayer intention. As with all change, this transformation to a twenty-first century apostolate after 175 years of deeply seated history has not been without sometimes painful growing pains. We thank all our readers and members for their cooperation, patience, and prayers.

This ministry is now a worldwide prayer network, responding to the challenges that confront humanity and the Church's mission as expressed in the pope's monthly intentions. In praying with these intentions, we extend our gaze to the whole world and enter personally into the joys and hopes, the pains and sufferings of our brothers and sisters everywhere.

The reflections in this volume are written by Doug Leonard, our former executive director, and can serve as an excellent adjunct to the Pope's Worldwide Prayer Network's practices of making a daily offering, pausing for recollection at noon, and performing self-examination in the evening. We at the Pope's Worldwide Prayer Network regional offices for Canada and the United States would especially like to thank Fr. Richard Buhler, S.J., of the Manresa Jesuit Retreat House in Convent, Louisiana, for reviewing this work.

Oremus!

Fr. William Blazek, S.J.
Regional Director
for US and Canada
Pope's Worldwide
Prayer Network

HOW TO USE THIS BOOK

Advent is all about waiting for Jesus Christ. The gospel readings of Advent make us mindful of three ways we await Jesus—past, present, and future. First, we remember and accompany Mary, Joseph, and the newborn Jesus. Second, we prepare for the celebration of his birth this Christmas so that the day doesn't pass us by with just meaningless words and worthless presents. Third, we anticipate the second coming of Jesus Christ, who will come in power and glory for everyone to see and establish his kingdom of peace and justice upon the earth.

Christ is born, and we follow him in exile and in those joyful early years with the Holy Family. We are blessed, but we are challenged, too, to understand the ways of God and how we personally may understand and respond to them now.

One of the ways we can better understand and respond to the Lord during this holy season of Advent is by rediscovering, along with Christians all over the world, a powerful, ancient form of prayer known as sacred reading (*lectio divina*). What better way to deepen one's friendship with Jesus Christ, the Word of God, than by prayerfully encountering him in the daily gospel? This book will set you on a personal prayer journey with Jesus.

Sacred Reading takes up this ancient practice of lectio divina in order to help you to engage the words of the daily gospel, guided by the Holy Spirit. As you read and pray this way, you may find—as many others have—that the Lord speaks to you in intimate and surprising ways. The reason for this is simple: as we open our hearts to Jesus, he opens his heart to us.

St. Paul prays beautifully for his readers:

> For this reason I bow my knees before the Father, from whom every family in heaven and on earth takes its name. I pray that, according to the riches of his glory, he may grant that you may be strengthened in your inner being with power through his Spirit, and that Christ may dwell in your hearts through faith, as you are being rooted and grounded in love. I pray that you may have the power to comprehend, with all the saints, what is the breadth and length and height and depth, and to know the love of Christ that surpasses knowledge, so that you may be filled with all the fullness of God. (Eph 3:14–19)

This book will set you on a personal prayer journey with Jesus from the first day of Advent through Epiphany Sunday. Each weekday reflection begins with the date, and some include a reference to the solemnity, feast, or sometimes a memorial on that day for which there is a special lectionary gospel reading. When these are indicated, the regular lectionary gospel reading for that day has been replaced with the gospel reading used to celebrate the solemnity or feast. Sunday reflections include both the date and its place in the liturgical calendar; any Sunday reading that includes a reference to a feast day rather than its place in the liturgical calendar uses the gospel reading for the feast day. For the sake of simplicity, other feast days are not cited when their gospel reading has not been used.

In prayerful reading of the daily gospels you join your prayers with those of believers all over the world. Following the readings for Advent and the Christmas season, each day you will be invited to reflect on the

gospel text for the day, following six simple but profound steps:

1. Know that God is present
with you and ready to converse.

At all times God is everywhere, including where you
are at this very moment. The human mind is incapa-
ble of fully grasping the mystery of God, but we do
know some things about God from scripture. God is
the transcendent ground of all being, invisible, eternal,
and infinite in power. God is love, with infinite love
for you and me. God is one with and revealed through
the Word, Jesus Christ, who became flesh. Through
him all things were made, and by him and for him
all things subsist. Jesus is the way, the truth, and the
life. He says that those who know him also know his
Father. Through the Passion, Death, and Resurrection
of Jesus, we are reconciled with God. If we believe in
Jesus Christ, we become the sons and daughters of
almighty God.

God gives us the Holy Spirit to lead us to truth and
understanding. The Holy Spirit also gives us power
to live obediently to the teachings of Jesus. The Holy
Spirit draws us to prayer and works in us as we pray.
No wonder we come into God's presence with gladness. All God's ways are good and beautiful. We can
get to know God better by encountering God in the
Word, Jesus himself.

The prompt prayer at the beginning of each day's
reading is just that—a prompt, something to get you
started. In fact, all the elements in the process of sacred
reading are meant to prompt you to your own conversations with God. After reading the prompt, feel free
to continue to pray in your own words: respond in
your own way, pray in your own way, and hear God

speaking to you personally. Your goal is to make sacred reading your own prayer time each day.

2. Read the gospel.

The entire Bible is the Word of God, but the gospels (Matthew, Mark, Luke, and John) specifically tell the Good News about Jesus Christ. Throughout the Church year, the daily gospel readings during Mass will come from all four gospels. Sacred reading concentrates on praying with the daily gospels. These readings contain the story of Jesus' life, his teachings, his works, his Passion and Death on the Cross, his Resurrection on the third day, and his Ascension into heaven.

The gospels interpret Jesus' ministry for us. Much more, by the Holy Spirit, we can find in the gospels the very person of Jesus Christ. Prayerful reading of the daily gospel is an opportunity to draw close to the Lord—Father, Son, and Holy Spirit. As we pray with the gospels, we can be transformed by the grace of God—enlightened, strengthened, and moved. Seek to read the gospel with a complete openness to what God is saying to you. Many who pray with the gospel recommend rereading it several times.

3. Notice what you think and feel as you read the gospel.

Sacred reading can involve every faculty—mind, heart, emotions, soul, spirit, sensations, imagination, and much more—though usually not all at once. Different passages touch different keys in us. Sometimes we may laugh. Sometimes we may need to stop and worship before we continue. Sometimes we will be puzzled, amazed, stung, abashed, reminded of something lovely, or reminded of something we had wanted to forget.

Seek to feel all of your emotions as you read. Apply your intellect, too. You will confront problems of context and exegesis on a daily basis. That's okay. Sometimes you may experience very little. That's okay, too. God is at work anyway. Give yourself to the gospel and take from it what is there for you each day.

Most important, notice what in particular jumps out at you, whatever it may be. It may be a word, a phrase, a character, an image, a pattern, an emotion, a sensation—some arrow to your heart. Whatever it is, pay attention to it, because the Holy Spirit is using it to accomplish something in you.

Sometimes a particular gospel repeats during the liturgical year of the Church. To pray through the same gospel even on successive days presents no problem whatsoever to your sacred reading. Saint Ignatius of Loyola, founder of the Jesuits and author of *The Spiritual Exercises*, actually recommends repeated meditation on passages of scripture. Read in the Spirit, gospel passages have unlimited potential to reveal to us the truths we are ready to receive. For the receptive soul, the Word of God has boundless power to illuminate and transform the prayerful believer.

4. Pray as you are led for yourself and others.

Praying is just talking with God. Believe God hears you. Believe God will answer you. Believe God knows what you need even before you ask. Jesus says so in the gospel. So, your conversation with God can go far beyond asking for things. You may thank, praise, worship, rejoice, mourn, explain, question, reveal your fears, seek understanding, or ask forgiveness. Your conversation with God has no limits. God is the ideal conversationalist. God wants to spend much time with you.

Being human, we can't help being self-absorbed, but praying is not just about our own needs. We are often moved by the gospel to pray for others. Often we will remember our loved ones in prayer. Sometimes we will be led to pray for someone who has hurt us. Sometimes we are moved to pray for a class of people in need, wherever they are in the world, such as for persecuted Christians, refugees, the mentally ill, the rich, teachers, the unborn, or the lonely.

We may also pray with the universal Church by praying for the pope's prayer intentions. Those intentions are entrusted to the Pope's Worldwide Prayer Network and are available through its website and its annual and monthly leaflets. You may get your own copy of this year's papal prayer intentions by contacting the Pope's Worldwide Prayer Network, which has more than thirty-five million members worldwide. Jesus asked us to unite in prayer, promising that the Father would grant us whatever we ask for in his name.

5. *Listen to Jesus.*

Jesus the Good Shepherd speaks to his own sheep, who hear his voice (see Jn 10:27). The passages in step five are words I felt impressed upon my heart as I prayed with these readings. I included them in order to help you listen for whatever it is the Lord might be saying to you.

This listening is a most wonderful time in your sacred reading prayer experience. Jesus speaks to all in the gospels, but in your sacred reading prayer experience he can now speak exclusively to you. If you can, write down what he says to you and reread his words during the day. Put all of Jesus' words to you in a folder or keep a spiritual notebook. Believers through the ages have recorded the words of Jesus to them, holy mystics and ordinary believers alike.

It takes faith to hear the voice of Jesus. This faith will grow as you practice listening. Ideally, we will learn to hear what Jesus is saying to us all day long—as we face difficult situations perhaps. Listening to the voice of Jesus is practicing the presence of God. As St. Paul said, "In him we live and move and have our being" (Acts 17:28).

St. Ignatius of Loyola called this conversation with Jesus *colloquy*. That word simply means that two or more people are talking. St. Ignatius even urges us to include the saints in our prayer conversations. We believe in the Communion of Saints. If you have a patron saint, don't be afraid to talk to him or her. In her autobiography, St. Thérèse of Lisieux, who was a member of the Apostleship of Prayer, describes how she spoke often with Mary and Joseph, as well as with Jesus.

6. *Ask God to show you how to live today.*

Pope Benedict XVI commented that sacred reading is not complete without a call to action; something in our praying leads us to do something in our day. Perhaps we find an opportunity to serve, to love, to give, to lead, or to do something good for someone else. Perhaps we find occasion to repent, to forgive, to ask forgiveness, to make amends. Open your heart to anything God might want you to do. Try to keep the conversation with God going all day long.

"Ask God to show you how to live today" is the last step of the sacred reading prayer time, but that doesn't mean you need to end it there. Keep it going. You may drift off in the presence of God, lose attention, or even fall asleep, but you can come back. God is always present, seeking to love you and to be loved. God is always seeking to lead us to green pastures. God is our strength, our rock, our ever-present help in time of trouble. God is full of mercy, ready to forgive us again and again. God sees us through very difficult times. God heals us. God gives his life to us constantly. God is our Maker, Father, Mother, Lover, Servant, Savior, and Friend. We know that from the gospel. He is an inexhaustible spring of blessing and holiness in our innermost selves. The sanctification of our souls is God's work, not our own.

As you read, ask the Holy Spirit to lead you in this process. With genuine faith, open yourself to respond to the Word and the Spirit, and your relationship with Jesus will continue to deepen and to grow just as the infant Jesus grew within the womb of the Blessed Mother. This in turn will lead you to share the love of Christ with all those you encounter—just as the Blessed Mother draws all those who encounter her directly to her Son.

Other Resources to Help You

These Sacred Reading resources, including both the seasonal books and the annual prayer book, are enriched by the spirituality of the Pope's Worldwide Prayer Network, formerly known as the Apostleship of Prayer. Since 1844, our mission has been to encourage Catholics to pray each day for the good of the world, the Church, and the prayer intentions of the Holy Father. In particular, we encourage Christians to respond to the loving gift of Jesus Christ by making a daily offering of themselves. As we give him our hearts, we ask that he may make them like his own heart, full of love, mercy, and peace.

These booklets may be used in small groups or as a handy individual resource for those who want a special way to draw close to Christ during Advent. If you enjoy these reflections and would like to continue this prayerful reading throughout the year, pick up a copy of the *Sacred Reading* annual prayer guide at the website of the Pope's Worldwide Prayer Network or avemariapress.com. These annual books offer a personal prayer experience that can be adapted to meet your particular needs. For example, some choose to continue to reflect in writing, either in the book or in a separate journal or notebook, to create a record of their spiritual journey for the entire year. Others supplement their daily reading from the book with the daily videos and other online resources available through the Pope's Worldwide Prayer Network.

For more information about the Pope's Worldwide Prayer Network and about the other resources we have developed to help men and women cultivate habits of daily prayer, visit our website at popesprayerusa.net.

FIRST WEEK OF ADVENT

A dvent is the time we are given to welcome the Lord who comes to encounter us, and also to verify our longing for God, to look forward and prepare ourselves for Christ's return. He will return to us in the celebration of Christmas, when we will remember his historic coming in the humility of the human condition, but he enters our heart each time we are willing to receive him, and he will come again at the end of time to "judge the living and the dead." Therefore, we must always be vigilant and await the Lord with the hope of encountering him.

Pope Francis
December 3, 2017

THE POPE'S MONTHLY PRAYER INTENTION FOR DECEMBER 2018

That people, who are involved in the service and transmission of faith, may find in their dialogue with culture a language suited to the conditions of the present time.

Sunday, December 2, 2018
First Sunday of Advent

Know that God is present with you and ready to converse.

Many of us learned as children that God is everywhere. St. Ignatius taught his followers to seek God in all things. So we turn to God's Word, authored by the Holy Spirit, who is One with the Father and the Son, Jesus the Messiah. God is here now, ready to speak to us.

When you are ready, lift your heart to God and receive God in the Word.

Read the gospel: Luke 21:25–28, 34–36.

Jesus said, "There will be signs in the sun, the moon, and the stars, and on the earth distress among nations confused by the roaring of the sea and the waves. People will faint from fear and foreboding of what is coming upon the world, for the powers of the heavens will be shaken. Then they will see 'the Son of Man coming in a cloud' with power and great glory. Now when these things begin to take place, stand up and raise your heads, because your redemption is drawing near. . . .

"Be on guard so that your hearts are not weighed down with dissipation and drunkenness and the worries of this life, and that day does not catch you unexpectedly, like a trap. For it will come upon all who live on the face of the whole earth. Be alert at all times, praying that you may have the strength to escape all these things that will take place, and to stand before the Son of Man."

Notice what you think and feel as you read the gospel.

The gospel asks us to take the long view in our lives, for the ultimate purpose is to live with God forever. In the meantime, we will be buffeted in our daily lives, sometimes terribly and sometimes more gently. Jesus asks us to trust in God's purposes for ourselves and for all people, to stay alert, and to pray.

Pray as you are led for yourself and others.

"I will be patient and alert, Lord, as I trust you to work in my life and with my loved ones. I pray specifically for these . . ." (Continue in your own words.)

Listen to Jesus.

I am glad you have come near to me today, beloved. I will direct your steps as you learn to trust me in everything. What else is Jesus saying to you?

Ask God to show you how to live today.

"Teach me how to listen to you and walk in your presence all day long and for my whole life. Thank you. Amen."

Monday, December 3, 2018

**Know that God is present with
you and ready to converse.**

"Glory to you, Lord. I am grateful for you now. Open me to your holy Word."

Read the gospel: Matthew 8:5–11.

When Jesus entered Capernaum, a centurion came to him, appealing to him and saying, "Lord, my servant is lying at home paralyzed, in terrible distress." And he said to him, "I will come and cure him." The centurion answered, "Lord, I am not worthy to have you come under my roof; but only speak the word, and my servant will be healed. For I also am a man under authority, with soldiers under me; and I say to one, 'Go,' and he goes, and to another, 'Come,' and he comes, and to my slave, 'Do this,' and the slave does it." When Jesus heard him, he was amazed and said to those who followed him, "Truly I tell you, in no one in Israel have I found such faith. I tell you, many will come from east and west and will eat with Abraham and Isaac and Jacob in the kingdom of heaven."

**Notice what you think and feel
as you read the gospel.**

The Roman centurion has all the qualities Jesus loves. It doesn't matter that he is not a Jew. He has faith, he loves his servant, and he is very humble. Jesus says, to our joy, that many from the east and the west will enter the kingdom of heaven.

Pray as you are led for yourself and others.

"Lord, I long to come in to your kingdom with your chosen from every nation. I pray now for people I know who need your healing . . ." (Continue in your own words.)

Listen to Jesus.

Come to me in faith as the centurion did. You will please me, and I will give you my life. Pray for others with compassion, for it is the quality of your compassion that makes your prayer powerful. What else is Jesus saying to you?

Ask God to show you how to live today.

"Jesus, your way is so simple, so pure. Give me grace to walk in it today. Thank you. Amen."

Tuesday, December 4, 2018

Know that God is present with you and ready to converse.

"I rejoice in your presence, Almighty God and Father. Let me be filled with your Spirit and your Word."

Read the gospel: Luke 10:21–24.

At that same hour Jesus rejoiced in the Holy Spirit and said, "I thank you, Father, Lord of heaven and earth, because you have hidden these things from the wise and the intelligent and have revealed them to infants; yes, Father, for such was your gracious will. All things have been handed over to me by my Father; and no one knows who the Son is except the Father, or who the Father is except the Son and anyone to whom the Son chooses to reveal him."

Then turning to the disciples, Jesus said to them privately, "Blessed are the eyes that see what you see! For I tell you that many prophets and kings desired to see what you see, but did not see it, and to hear what you hear, but did not hear it."

Notice what you think and feel as you read the gospel.

Jesus prays to his Father, thanking him for revealing the Son to people—not to the wise and intelligent but to infants. Likewise, the Son has power to reveal himself and the Father. We are blessed beyond all we can imagine to have loving knowledge of God.

Pray as you are led for yourself and others.

"Lord, I reject all my pride and come to you as a child. Let me please you in that. I pray also for those you have given me . . ." (Continue in your own words.)

Listen to Jesus.

I love you, my child. Pray for those who do not yet know me. They will come to me. What else is Jesus saying to you?

Ask God to show you how to live today.

"Lord, I humbly ask to know you and the work you have for me each day, this day. I seek to follow you. Amen."

Wednesday, December 5, 2018

Know that God is present with you and ready to converse.

"Lord, you have come to me today to heal and feed me. Thank you."

Read the gospel: Matthew 15:29–37.

After Jesus had left that place, he passed along the Sea of Galilee, and he went up the mountain, where he sat down. Great crowds came to him, bringing with them the lame, the maimed, the blind, the mute, and many others. They put them at his feet, and he cured them, so that the crowd was amazed when they saw the mute speaking, the maimed whole, the lame walking, and the blind seeing. And they praised the God of Israel.

Then Jesus called his disciples to him and said, "I have compassion for the crowd, because they have been with me now for three days and have nothing to eat; and I do not want to send them away hungry, for they might faint on the way." The disciples said to him, "Where are we to get enough bread in the desert to feed so great a crowd?" Jesus asked them, "How many loaves have you?" They said, "Seven, and a few small fish." Then ordering the crowd to sit down on the ground, he took the seven loaves and the fish; and after giving thanks he broke them and gave them to the disciples, and the disciples gave them to the crowds. And all of them ate and were filled; and they took up the broken pieces left over, seven baskets full.

Notice what you think and feel as you read the gospel.

Those who need healing are brought to the feet of Jesus, and he heals them. The very crowd that brought the lame, the blind, and the mute to Jesus are yet amazed when he heals them. And then, though they don't think to ask for something as simple as food, Jesus knows their needs and provides for them out of love. What are our expectations as we come to Jesus?

Pray as you are led for yourself and others.

"I want to show you faith, Lord—faith to follow you, trusting you for healing and sharing your love with others. I pray now for these . . ." (Continue in your own words.)

Listen to Jesus.

Because you call out to me, I give you healing today, dear disciple. Receive me in your heart. What else is Jesus saying to you?

Ask God to show you how to live today.

"Let me draw near and stay near to you all day, Lord. Help me serve you today. Amen."

Thursday, December 6, 2018

Know that God is present with you and ready to converse.

"Thank you for visiting me as I approach your Word, Lord. I will attend to you."

Read the gospel: Matthew 7:21, 24–27.

Jesus said to his disciples, "Not everyone who says to me, 'Lord, Lord,' will enter the kingdom of heaven, but only one who does the will of my Father in heaven. . . . Everyone then who hears these words of mine and acts on them will be like a wise man who built his house on rock. The rain fell, the floods came, and the winds blew and beat on that house, but it did not fall, because it had been founded on rock. And everyone who hears these words of mine and does not act on them will be like a foolish man who built his house on sand. The rain fell, and the floods came, and the winds blew and beat against that house, and it fell—and great was its fall!"

Notice what you think and feel as you read the gospel.

Jesus says that the Word of God has no saving effect unless the one who hears it acts upon it. It is up to us to speak and act in response to the Word of God. If we do the will of the Father, we will enter the kingdom.

Pray as you are led for yourself and others.

"Jesus, you are my rock; let me build upon you, seeking to do the will of God. Let me serve you and others well . . ." (Continue in your own words.)

Listen to Jesus.

If you rely on me, you will see changes in your life. You will grow stronger in faith, hope, and love, and your service will glorify God. What else is Jesus saying to you?

Ask God to show you how to live today.

"Lord, give me eyes to see you and let me walk with you all day, Lord. I seek to act in your will. Amen."

Friday, December 7, 2018

Know that God is present with you and ready to converse.

"Lord, teach me by your Word today. You are the same yesterday, today, and forever."

Read the gospel: Matthew 9:27–31.

As Jesus went on from there, two blind men followed him, crying loudly, "Have mercy on us, Son of David!" When he entered the house, the blind men came to him; and Jesus said to them, "Do you believe that I am able to do this?" They said to him, "Yes, Lord." Then he touched their eyes and said, "According to your faith let it be done to you." And their eyes were opened. Then Jesus sternly ordered them, "See that no one knows of this." But they went away and spread the news about him throughout that district.

Notice what you think and feel as you read the gospel.

Jesus heals the blind men according to their faith. Because of their faith, their eyes are opened. In their enthusiasm, they fail to obey Jesus, and they tell everyone about him.

Pray as you are led for yourself and others.

"Lord, my own faith is willing but weak. Let me reach out to you with what faith you have given me and seek healing in all the parts needing it. I pray also for the faith of others who need you . . ." (Continue in your own words.)

Listen to Jesus.

Dear servant. I grant you what you ask. Cling to me, and know I love you. What else is Jesus saying to you?

Ask God to show you how to live today.

"I resolve today to act upon the faith and love you give me, serving my neighbor. Thank you, Lord. Amen."

Saturday, December 8, 2018
Immaculate Conception of
the Blessed Virgin Mary

Know that God is present with you and ready to converse.

"Lord, instruct me by your Word, and let it be done to me accordingly."

Read the gospel: Luke 1:26–38.

In the sixth month the angel Gabriel was sent by God to a town in Galilee called Nazareth, to a virgin engaged to a man whose name was Joseph, of the house of David. The virgin's name was Mary. And he came to her and said, "Greetings, favored one! The Lord is with you." But she was much perplexed by his words and pondered what sort of greeting this might be. The angel said to her, "Do not be afraid, Mary, for you have found favor with God. And now, you will conceive in your womb and bear a son, and you will name him Jesus. He will be great, and will be called the Son of the Most High, and the Lord God will give to him the throne of his ancestor David. He will reign over the house of Jacob forever, and of his kingdom there will be no end." Mary said to the angel, "How can this be, since I am a virgin?" The angel said to her,

"The Holy Spirit will come upon you, and the power of the Most High will overshadow you; therefore the child to be born will be holy; he will be called Son of God. And now, your relative Elizabeth in her old age has also conceived a son; and this is the sixth month for her who was said to be barren. For nothing will be impossible with God." Then Mary said, "Here am I, the servant of the Lord; let it be with me according to your word." Then the angel departed from her.

Notice what you think and feel as you read the gospel.

The angel appears to tell Mary what God will do with her. Gabriel does not ask for Mary's permission, but after hearing his words, Mary agrees. She must have barely comprehended the marvelous prophecy, but she has faith and submits to the will of God.

Pray as you are led for yourself and others.

"I bless Mary for her obedience and mildness. Let me have the spirit of our Mother that I may serve others as she did . . ." (Continue in your own words.)

Listen to Jesus.

I thank you for your love for our Mother, mine and yours, for your faith has made you a child of God and a sibling to me. What else is Jesus saying to you?

Ask God to show you how to live today.

"Let me approach today with the simplicity and gentleness of Mary, Lord. Help me to do your will as generously as she did. Amen."

SECOND WEEK OF ADVENT

The Savior whom we await is able to transform our life with his grace, with the power of the Holy Spirit, with the power of love. The Holy Spirit, in fact, infuses our hearts with God's love, the inexhaustible source of purification, of new life and freedom. The Virgin Mary fully lived this reality, allowing herself to be "baptized" by the Holy Spirit who inundated her with his power. May she, who prepared for the coming of Christ with the totality of her existence, help us to follow her example, and may she guide our steps to the coming Lord.

Pope Francis
December 10, 2017

Sunday, December 9, 2018
Second Sunday of Advent

Know that God is present with you and ready to converse.

"Lord, you are present with me in the words John the Baptist proclaimed before your public ministry. Glory to you."

Read the gospel: Luke 3:1–6.

In the fifteenth year of the reign of Emperor Tiberius, when Pontius Pilate was governor of Judea, and Herod was ruler of Galilee, and his brother Philip ruler of the region of Ituraea and Trachonitis, and Lysanias ruler of Abilene, during the high-priesthood of Annas and Caiaphas, the word of God came to John son of Zechariah in the wilderness. He went into all the region around the Jordan, proclaiming a baptism of repentance for the forgiveness of sins, as it is written in the book of the words of the prophet Isaiah,

> "The voice of one crying out in the wilderness:
> 'Prepare the way of the Lord,
>   make his paths straight.
> Every valley shall be filled,
>   and every mountain and hill shall be made
>   low,
>   and the crooked shall be made straight,
>   and the rough ways made smooth;
> and all flesh shall see the salvation of God.'"

Notice what you think and feel as you read the gospel.

The evangelist goes to great pains to locate these events in secular history—he refers to specific worldly authorities to pinpoint place and time—to point out that "the salvation of God" was not just an ethereal prophecy but the concrete, tangible, and real fulfillment of the Old Testament prophecy.

Pray as you are led for yourself and others.

"John spoke the truth to friends and enemies alike. He spoke of you, my Jesus. Let me imitate John in your service . . ." (Continue in your own words.)

Listen to Jesus.

You are seeing the salvation of the Lord, my child, as you turn to me and trust in me. I wash away your sins when you repent. Bear good fruit. Pray for those who need your prayers. What else is Jesus saying to you?

Ask God to show you how to live today.

"My Lord, my Savior. Baptize me with your Holy Spirit that I may have power to serve. Amen."

Monday, December 10, 2018

Know that God is present with you and ready to converse.

"Lord, you have power to forgive sins and to heal. I seek forgiveness and healing through your Word."

Read the gospel: Luke 5:17–26.

One day, while Jesus was teaching, Pharisees and teachers of the law were sitting nearby (they had come

from every village of Galilee and Judea and from Jerusalem); and the power of the Lord was with him to
heal. Just then some men came, carrying a paralyzed
man on a bed. They were trying to bring him in and lay
him before Jesus; but finding no way to bring him in
because of the crowd, they went up on the roof and let
him down with his bed through the tiles into the mid-
dle of the crowd in front of Jesus. When he saw their
faith, he said, "Friend, your sins are forgiven you."
Then the scribes and the Pharisees began to question,
"Who is this who is speaking blasphemies? Who can
forgive sins but God alone?" When Jesus perceived
their questionings, he answered them, "Why do you
raise such questions in your hearts? Which is easier, to
say, 'Your sins are forgiven you,' or to say, 'Stand up
and walk'? But so that you may know that the Son of
Man has authority on earth to forgive sins"—he said
to the one who was paralyzed—"I say to you, stand up
and take your bed and go to your home." Immediately
he stood up before them, took what he had been lying
on, and went to his home, glorifying God. Amazement
seized all of them, and they glorified God and were
filled with awe, saying, "We have seen strange things
today."

Notice what you think and feel
as you read the gospel.

His devoted friends lower the paralyzed man on a
bed before Jesus. The Lord forgives the man before
the crowd, which included scribes and Pharisees who
question his authority to forgive, for only God can forgive sins. Jesus asserts his authority and heals the par-
alytic, who takes up his bed and goes home, glorifying
God. Then all of them, filled with awe, glorify God. Did
the scribes and Pharisees join them?

Pray as you are led for yourself and others.

"Lord, I glorify you for your authority to forgive and to heal, for I need both. Make me well in body and soul to serve you and others, including . . ." (Continue in your own words.)

Listen to Jesus.

I receive you, dear child. Turn from sin. I will help you. What else is Jesus saying to you?

Ask God to show you how to live today.

"Jesus, I believe you work wonders every day. Show me how you can use me to help others in need. Let me please you today. Amen."

Tuesday, December 11, 2018

Know that God is present with you and ready to converse.

"Jesus, you are the Word of God. Let me not go astray."

Read the gospel: Matthew 18:12–14.

Jesus asked his disciples, "What do you think? If a shepherd has a hundred sheep, and one of them has gone astray, does he not leave the ninety-nine on the mountains and go in search of the one that went astray? And if he finds it, truly I tell you, he rejoices over it more than over the ninety-nine that never went astray. So it is not the will of your Father in heaven that one of these little ones should be lost."

Notice what you think and feel
as you read the gospel.

Jesus and his Father seek and rescue the lost sheep, one by one. God wants to bring all people to him.

Pray as you are led for yourself and others.

"Loving Shepherd, find me. I long to make you happy by being found, redeemed, and returned to the fold. I pray for all the lost sheep . . ." (Continue in your own words.)

Listen to Jesus.

God's love is endless, little one. He saves all the little ones he loves. What else is Jesus saying to you?

Ask God to show you how to live today.

"What can I do to find and feed your sheep, Lord? I offer myself now. Amen."

Wednesday, December 12, 2018
Our Lady of Guadalupe

Know that God is present with
you and ready to converse.

"Thank you for your work in the Americas, Lord. Let your Lady continue to turn hearts to you."

Read the gospel: Luke 1:26–38.

In the sixth month the angel Gabriel was sent by God to a town in Galilee called Nazareth, to a virgin engaged to a man whose name was Joseph, of the house of David. The virgin's name was Mary. And he came to her and said, "Greetings, favored one! The Lord is with you." But she was much perplexed by his words and pondered what sort of greeting this might be. The angel said to her, "Do not be afraid, Mary, for you have found favor with God. And now, you will conceive in your womb and bear a son, and you will name him Jesus. He will be great, and will be called the Son of the Most High, and the Lord God will give to him the throne of his ancestor David. He will reign over the house of Jacob forever, and of his kingdom there will be no end." Mary said to the angel, "How can this be, since I am a virgin?" The angel said to her, "The Holy Spirit will come upon you, and the power of the Most High will overshadow you; therefore the child to be born will be holy; he will be called Son of God. And now, your relative Elizabeth in her old age has also conceived a son; and this is the sixth month for her who was said to be barren. For nothing will be impossible with God." Then Mary said, "Here am I, the servant of the Lord; let it be with me according to your word." Then the angel departed from her.

Notice what you think and feel as you read the gospel.

Is it any wonder that Mary questions the angel Gabriel about the astonishing things God has planned to do for her and through her? In her humility, though, she entrusts herself and her future to God.

Pray as you are led for yourself and others.

"Dear Trinity of Love, I entrust myself to your mighty and holy will. I will not allow myself to be distressed by the threats to my peace in the world. You are Lord, and I give myself and my loved ones to you . . ." (Continue in your own words.)

Listen to Jesus.

Yes, trust me with a peaceful spirit, dear friend and child. Let me operate in your life. I will give you what you need and keep you safe for everlasting life. What else is Jesus saying to you?

Ask God to show you how to live today.

"How may I spread your gospel of peace to others, Lord? Give me the power of your Spirit. Amen."

Thursday, December 13, 2018

Know that God is present with you and ready to converse.

"Jesus, give me ears to hear your Word today. Show me how to follow you."

Read the gospel: Matthew 11:11–15.

Jesus said, "Truly I tell you, among those born of women no one has arisen greater than John the Baptist; yet the least in the kingdom of heaven is greater than he. From the days of John the Baptist until now the kingdom of heaven has suffered violence, and the violent take it by force. For all the prophets and the law prophesied until John came; and if you are willing to accept it, he is Elijah who is to come. Let anyone with ears listen!"

Notice what you think and feel as you read the gospel.

In praising John the Baptist, Jesus unites John's ministry with his own, validating John's baptism and calling his disciples to follow him.

Pray as you are led for yourself and others.

"God, I would rejoice to be the least in your kingdom. Let me come to you, Lord, and lead also those you have given me . . ." (Continue in your own words.)

Listen to Jesus.

I am with you, dear servant. I am leading you. With me you are safe. What else is Jesus saying to you?

Ask God to show you how to live today.

"You are the Messiah, Jesus. I glorify you and thank you for your great promises to me. Make me worthy of your kingdom, starting today. Amen."

Friday, December 14, 2018

Know that God is present with you and ready to converse.

"Jesus, help me to recognize your will for me as I read your Word. Let me receive it as you mean it for me. Teach me now."

Read the gospel: Matthew 11:16–19.

Jesus said, "But to what will I compare this generation? It is like children sitting in the marketplaces and calling to one another,

> 'We played the flute for you, and you did not dance;
> we wailed, and you did not mourn.'

For John came neither eating nor drinking, and they say, 'He has a demon'; the Son of Man came eating and drinking, and they say, 'Look, a glutton and a

drunkard, a friend of tax collectors and sinners!' Yet
wisdom is vindicated by her deeds."

Notice what you think and feel as you read the gospel.

Jesus considers the contrasting preaching styles of
John the Baptist and himself, and he laments those
who have rejected both. Some people you just can't
please; they will look for problems because they do
not want to come to God.

Pray as you are led for yourself and others.

"Jesus, you speak of wisdom and its connection to
one's deeds. Give me the wisdom to do your will,
and give those who reject you the wisdom to receive
you . . ." (Continue in your own words.)

Listen to Jesus.

*I am pleased you ask for wisdom, my child. I am the wisdom
of God, and you will find endless wisdom in me. Be patient
with yourself and wait patiently for God. I will bless you
with wisdom.* What else is Jesus saying to you?

Ask God to show you how to live today.

"Thank you for your constant care of me, dear Jesus.
I want to cling to you in everything, today, tomorrow,
and always. Amen."

Saturday, December 15, 2018

Know that God is present with you and ready to converse.

"God, you reveal yourself to human beings, often in mysterious ways. Lord, open my mind and heart to understand your Word."

Read the gospel: Matthew 17:9–13.

As they were coming down the mountain, Jesus ordered them, "Tell no one about the vision until after the Son of Man has been raised from the dead." And the disciples asked him, "Why, then, do the scribes say that Elijah must come first?" He replied, "Elijah is indeed coming and will restore all things; but I tell you that Elijah has already come, and they did not recognize him, but they did to him whatever they pleased. So also the Son of Man is about to suffer at their hands." Then the disciples understood that he was speaking to them about John the Baptist.

Notice what you think and feel as you read the gospel.

Jesus' disciples question him about what they have just seen: the Transfiguration, when Jesus appeared in glory before them speaking to Moses and Elijah. They speak of some Messianic prophesies foretelling the coming of Elijah before the Messiah. Jesus seems to consider that Elijah has indeed come in the person of John the Baptist, who was killed, and he says that he too will suffer at the hands of the authorities.

Pray as you are led for yourself and others.

"Jesus, you speak of the suffering of the prophets and yourself. As your disciple, I expect to suffer as well, and I seek to accept it with obedience, for I know all things are for my good. I pray also for others who suffer, including . . ." (Continue in your own words.)

Listen to Jesus.

Do not fear suffering, my child. Look to God in all things. What else is Jesus saying to you?

Ask God to show you how to live today.

"As I face my suffering today, Lord, I offer it all for the good of others, especially those who suffer and most especially those who may cause me to suffer. Amen."

THIRD WEEK OF ADVENT

Joy, prayer, and gratitude are three attitudes that prepare us to experience Christmas in an authentic way. . . . In this last period of the Season of Advent, let us entrust ourselves to the maternal intercession of the Virgin Mary. She is a "cause of our joy," not only because she begot Jesus but because she keeps directing us to him.

Pope Francis
December 17, 2017

Sunday, December 16, 2018
Third Sunday of Advent

Know that God is present with you and ready to converse.

"How wonderful are your ways, God. You are with me now."

Read the gospel: Luke 3:10–18.

And the crowds asked Jesus, "What then should we do?" In reply he said to them, "Whoever has two coats must share with anyone who has none; and whoever has food must do likewise." Even tax collectors came to be baptized, and they asked him, "Teacher, what should we do?" He said to them, "Collect no more than the amount prescribed for you." Soldiers also asked him, "And we, what should we do?" He said to them, "Do not extort money from anyone by threats or false accusation, and be satisfied with your wages."

As the people were filled with expectation, and all were questioning in their hearts concerning John, whether he might be the Messiah, John answered all of them by saying, "I baptize you with water; but one who is more powerful than I is coming; I am not worthy to untie the thong of his sandals. He will baptize you with the Holy Spirit and fire. His winnowing fork is in his hand, to clear his threshing floor and to gather the wheat into his granary; but the chaff he will burn with unquenchable fire."

So, with many other exhortations, he proclaimed the good news to the people.

Notice what you think and feel as you read the gospel.

Jesus teaches the people simple morality, based on justice, generosity, gentleness, and humility. The people are taken with him and his message. Might this be the Messiah John the Baptist spoke of who will baptize with the Holy Spirit and fire?

Pray as you are led for yourself and others.

"Lord, help me to practice morality in my own life. Baptize me with your Holy Spirit and fire so that I may give you glory in my service to you and others . . ." (Continue in your own words.)

Listen to Jesus.

You are right that simplicity is the key to good behavior and a good life. I am with you, dear servant. I send my Spirit upon you as you ask. What else is Jesus saying to you?

Ask God to show you how to live today.

"You are good to me, Lord. Strengthen me to perform my duty to God and others. Let my love for you impel me. Amen."

Monday, December 17, 2018

Know that God is present with you and ready to converse.

"Jesus, you are Son of God and Son of Man. Let me contemplate what it means that you took mortal flesh to confer everlasting life upon us. Open me to your Word, Lord."

Read the gospel: Matthew 1:1–17.

An account of the genealogy of Jesus the Messiah, the
son of David, the son of Abraham.

Abraham was the father of Isaac, and Isaac the
father of Jacob, and Jacob the father of Judah and his
brothers, and Judah the father of Perez and Zerah by
Tamar, and Perez the father of Hezron, and Hezron
the father of Aram, and Aram the father of Aminadab,
and Aminadab the father of Nahshon, and Nahshon
the father of Salmon, and Salmon the father of Boaz by
Rahab, and Boaz the father of Obed by Ruth, and Obed
the father of Jesse, and Jesse the father of King David.

And David was the father of Solomon by the wife
of Uriah, and Solomon the father of Rehoboam, and
Rehoboam the father of Abijah, and Abijah the father
of Asaph, and Asaph the father of Jehoshaphat, and
Jehoshaphat the father of Joram, and Joram the father
of Uzziah, and Uzziah the father of Jotham, and Jotham
the father of Ahaz, and Ahaz the father of Hezekiah,
and Hezekiah the father of Manasseh, and Manasseh
the father of Amos, and Amos the father of Josiah, and
Josiah the father of Jechoniah and his brothers, at the
time of the deportation to Babylon.

And after the deportation to Babylon: Jechoniah
was the father of Salathiel, and Salathiel the father of
Zerubbabel, and Zerubbabel the father of Abiud, and
Abiud the father of Eliakim, and Eliakim the father of
Azor, and Azor the father of Zadok, and Zadok the
father of Achim, and Achim the father of Eliud, and
Eliud the father of Eleazar, and Eleazar the father of
Matthan, and Matthan the father of Jacob, and Jacob
the father of Joseph the husband of Mary, of whom
Jesus was born, who is called the Messiah.

So all the generations from Abraham to David are
fourteen generations; and from David to the deportation to Babylon, fourteen generations; and from

the deportation to Babylon to the Messiah, fourteen generations.

Notice what you think and feel as you read the gospel.

Jesus the man was descended from people good and bad—such are the ways of the Lord in sending his Messiah. He shared our nature, yet he was without sin. Jesus' holiness and divinity in a vessel of flesh are essential for our redemption.

Pray as you are led for yourself and others.

"Lord, thank you for coming to us to save us. You are alive and working among us now. Come to me and save me from my sins. Come to those I pray for . . ." (Continue in your own words.)

Listen to Jesus.

As you come to me in prayer, my beloved, I work to prepare you for the kingdom of God. What else is Jesus saying to you?

Ask God to show you how to live today.

"Lord, inspire me to pray often. Glory to you, Redeemer. Amen."

Tuesday, December 18, 2018

Know that God is present with you and ready to converse.

"You know my heart, Lord. Let it be open now to your Word."

Read the gospel: Matthew 1:18–25.

Now the birth of Jesus the Messiah took place in this
way. When his mother Mary had been engaged to
Joseph, but before they lived together, she was found
to be with child from the Holy Spirit. Her husband
Joseph, being a righteous man and unwilling to expose
her to public disgrace, planned to dismiss her quietly.
But just when he had resolved to do this, an angel of
the Lord appeared to him in a dream and said, "Joseph,
son of David, do not be afraid to take Mary as your
wife, for the child conceived in her is from the Holy
Spirit. She will bear a son, and you are to name him
Jesus, for he will save his people from their sins." All
this took place to fulfill what had been spoken by the
Lord through the prophet:

> "Look, the virgin shall conceive and bear a son,
>   and they shall name him Emmanuel,"

which means, "God is with us." When Joseph awoke
from sleep, he did as the angel of the Lord commanded him; he took her as his wife, but had no marital
relations with her until she had borne a son; and he
named him Jesus.

Notice what you think and feel
as you read the gospel.

Joseph, a just man betrothed to Mary, here tries to deal
with the fact of her pregnancy. He wants to do the right
thing. An angel in a dream tells him what is going on
and what he should do. Joseph believes and obeys.

Pray as you are led for yourself and others.

"Lord, let me be open to all things that befall me, knowing they come from you. I am your servant, Lord . . ." (Continue in your own words.)

Listen to Jesus.

When you face problems or questions of direction, look to me, my servant. I will guide you into the godly way. What else is Jesus saying to you?

Ask God to show you how to live today.

"Jesus, speak to me always. Let me walk in your Holy Spirit today. Let me hear you more and more. Amen."

Wednesday, December 19, 2018

Know that God is present with you and ready to converse.

"Lord, your Word is true. Let me believe it in my heart, my soul, my mind. Your Spirit is present with me now."

Read the gospel: Luke 1:5–25.

In the days of King Herod of Judea, there was a priest named Zechariah, who belonged to the priestly order of Abijah. His wife was a descendant of Aaron, and her name was Elizabeth. Both of them were righteous before God, living blamelessly according to all the commandments and regulations of the Lord. But they had no children, because Elizabeth was barren, and both were getting on in years.

Once when he was serving as priest before God and his section was on duty, he was chosen by lot, according to the custom of the priesthood, to enter the sanctuary of the Lord and offer incense. Now at the time of the incense-offering, the whole assembly of the people was praying outside. Then there appeared to him an angel of the Lord, standing at the right side of the altar of incense. When Zechariah saw him, he was terrified; and fear overwhelmed him. But the angel said to him, "Do not be afraid, Zechariah, for your prayer has been heard. Your wife Elizabeth will bear you a son, and you will name him John. You will have joy and gladness, and many will rejoice at his birth, for he will be great in the sight of the Lord. He must never drink wine or strong drink; even before his birth he will be filled with the Holy Spirit. He will turn many of the people of Israel to the Lord their God. With the spirit and power of Elijah he will go before him, to turn the hearts of parents to their children, and the disobedient to the wisdom of the righteous, to make ready a people prepared for the Lord." Zechariah said to the angel, "How will I know that this is so? For I am an old man, and my wife is getting on in years." The angel replied, "I am Gabriel. I stand in the presence of God, and I have been sent to speak to you and to bring you this good news. But now, because you did not believe my words, which will be fulfilled in their time, you will become mute, unable to speak, until the day these things occur."

Meanwhile, the people were waiting for Zechariah, and wondered at his delay in the sanctuary. When he did come out, he could not speak to them, and they realized that he had seen a vision in the sanctuary. He kept motioning to them and remained unable to speak. When his time of service was ended, he went to his home.

After those days his wife Elizabeth conceived, and for five months she remained in seclusion. She said, "This is what the Lord has done for me when he looked favorably on me and took away the disgrace I have endured among my people."

Notice what you think and feel as you read the gospel.

While Mary believed Gabriel's announcement and Joseph believed the angel in the dream, Zechariah doubts Gabriel's announcement to him. How could this aged couple conceive a child, even if the child was to be a prophet of the Lord? But Elizabeth becomes pregnant with John the Baptist, who would be the forerunner of the Messiah.

Pray as you are led for yourself and others.

"Lord, fill me with faith as I await your coming. Let me trust in you in all my affairs. In the future with you I have nothing to fear. I pray for those in fear . . ." (Continue in your own words.)

Listen to Jesus.

You are right to trust me, child. I will do marvelous things in your life as you cling to me and seek to walk in all my ways. I love you. What else is Jesus saying to you?

Ask God to show you how to live today.

"Lord, let me, like Elizabeth, humbly and fearlessly proclaim all that God, in his grace, has done for me. Thank you. Amen."

Thursday, December 20, 2018

**Know that God is present with
you and ready to converse.**

"Let me magnify you, my Lord, in the same spirit as
your servant Mary."

Read the gospel: Luke 1:26–38.

In the sixth month the angel Gabriel was sent by
God to a town in Galilee called Nazareth, to a virgin
engaged to a man whose name was Joseph, of the
house of David. The virgin's name was Mary. And he
came to her and said, "Greetings, favored one! The
Lord is with you." But she was much perplexed by his
words and pondered what sort of greeting this might
be. The angel said to her, "Do not be afraid, Mary, for
you have found favor with God. And now, you will
conceive in your womb and bear a son, and you will
name him Jesus. He will be great, and will be called
the Son of the Most High, and the Lord God will give
to him the throne of his ancestor David. He will reign
over the house of Jacob forever, and of his kingdom
there will be no end." Mary said to the angel, "How
can this be, since I am a virgin?" The angel said to her,
"The Holy Spirit will come upon you, and the power
of the Most High will overshadow you; therefore the
child to be born will be holy; he will be called Son of
God. And now, your relative Elizabeth in her old age
has also conceived a son; and this is the sixth month
for her who was said to be barren. For nothing will be
impossible with God." Then Mary said, "Here am I, the
servant of the Lord; let it be with me according to your
word." Then the angel departed from her.

Notice what you think and feel as you read the gospel.

The angel emphasizes that Mary will have a child conceived by God. The Holy Spirit will come upon her, and the power of the Most High will overshadow her, and the child shall be called the Son of God. Mary must have been amazed, but she consents to God's will.

Pray as you are led for yourself and others.

"Lord, I worship you, for you are Almighty God, though flesh and blood like me. This is a mystery. I rejoice in you . . ." (Continue in your own words.)

Listen to Jesus.

Your trust and your joy in me are gifts I have given you. I am the Master, beloved, and my power shall never fail you, neither in this life or the next. You are mine. What else is Jesus saying to you?

Ask God to show you how to live today.

"Give me the strength and the grace, Lord, to be and do all you ask. Today let me look to your power and care. Let me serve you in others. Amen."

Friday, December 21, 2018

Know that God is present with you and ready to converse.

"I rejoice in your presence, Lord. Open my ears to hear your Word, Lord, then let me bless you."

Read the gospel: Luke 1:39–45.

In those days Mary set out and went with haste to a Judean town in the hill country, where she entered

the house of Zechariah and greeted Elizabeth. When
Elizabeth heard Mary's greeting, the child leapt in her
womb. And Elizabeth was filled with the Holy Spirit
and exclaimed with a loud cry, "Blessed are you among
women, and blessed is the fruit of your womb. And
why has this happened to me, that the mother of my
Lord comes to me? For as soon as I heard the sound
of your greeting, the child in my womb leapt for joy.
And blessed is she who believed that there would be
a fulfillment of what was spoken to her by the Lord."

Notice what you think and feel as you read the gospel.

There is great joy in two godly women, both pregnant
according to the purposes and power of God. Their
love for each other is evident. The Holy Spirit is present
in the pregnant women and the infants in their wombs.

Pray as you are led for yourself and others.

"Lord, with Mary and Elizabeth, I rejoice in you. Work
your purposes in my life and fill me with praise for
you. Do great things with me for your glory and the
good of others . . ." (Continue in your own words.)

Listen to Jesus.

*I have work for you too, my child, and you will know my
joy. You will serve me in love.* What else is Jesus saying
to you?

Ask God to show you how to live today.

"Help me to do well what you give me to do, Lord. I
offer all that I am and all that I have to you. Let God
be glorified. Amen."

Saturday, December 22, 2018

Know that God is present with you and ready to converse.

"God, open my heart to praise you. Let me learn praise by your Word."

Read the gospel: Luke 1:46–56.

And Mary said,

> "My soul magnifies the Lord,
>> and my spirit rejoices in God my Savior,
> for he has looked with favor on the lowliness of
>> his servant.
>> Surely, from now on all generations will call
>> me blessed;
> for the Mighty One has done great things for me,
>> and holy is his name.
> His mercy is for those who fear him
>> from generation to generation.
> He has shown strength with his arm;
>> he has scattered the proud in the thoughts of
>> their hearts.
> He has brought down the powerful from their
>> thrones,
>> and lifted up the lowly;
> he has filled the hungry with good things,
>> and sent the rich away empty.
> He has helped his servant Israel,
>> in remembrance of his mercy,
> according to the promise he made to our ancestors,
>> to Abraham and to his descendants forever."

And Mary remained with Elizabeth for about three months and then returned to her home.

Notice what you think and feel as you read the gospel.

Mary praises God for lifting up the lowly and putting down the haughty. God shows mercy to the needy and gathers them; the mighty he scatters.

Pray as you are led for yourself and others.

"Praise to you, O Lord, for you have done and still do what Mary proclaimed in her hymn of praise. Help me to walk in the steps of the lowly, praising you . . ." (Continue in your own words.)

Listen to Jesus.

The joy of the Lord is your strength, beloved. The things that swirl outside and inside need not take away your joy. Share it. What else is Jesus saying to you?

Ask God to show you how to live today.

"Your joy is like no other, Lord. Let me truly rejoice by the power of your Spirit, and I will share your joy with others today. Amen."

FOURTH WEEK OF ADVENT

In the Child of Bethlehem, God comes to meet us and make us active sharers in the life around us. He offers himself to us, so that we can take him into our arms, lift him, and embrace him. So that in him we will not be afraid to take into our arms, raise up, and embrace the thirsty, the stranger, the naked, the sick, the imprisoned. . . . In this Child, God invites us to be messengers of hope. He invites us to become sentinels for all those bowed down by the despair born of encountering so many closed doors. In this child, God makes us agents of his hospitality.

Pope Francis
December 24, 2017

Sunday, December 23, 2018
Fourth Sunday of Advent

Know that God is present with you and ready to converse.

"God, as you were present in Mary and Elizabeth, you are also present with me. I glorify you as I read your Word."

Read the gospel: Luke 1:39–45.

In those days Mary set out and went with haste to a Judean town in the hill country, where she entered the house of Zechariah and greeted Elizabeth. When Elizabeth heard Mary's greeting, the child leapt in her womb. And Elizabeth was filled with the Holy Spirit and exclaimed with a loud cry, "Blessed are you among women, and blessed is the fruit of your womb. And why has this happened to me, that the mother of my Lord comes to me? For as soon as I heard the sound of your greeting, the child in my womb leapt for joy. And blessed is she who believed that there would be a fulfillment of what was spoken to her by the Lord."

Notice what you think and feel as you read the gospel.

Elizabeth is aware that her younger cousin, Mary, is pregnant with the Lord. John the Baptist in Elizabeth's womb is already heralding the coming of the Messiah, and Elizabeth blesses Mary.

Pray as you are led for yourself and others.

"Thank you for giving me the example of these holy women who are serving your purposes with such joy and love. Make me like them, Jesus. I pray for joy and

love for all those you have given me . . ." (Continue in
your own words.)

Listen to Jesus.

*I knew you in the womb, child, and I loved you. I will that
you may love and serve God and then come into the eternal
kingdom.* What else is Jesus saying to you?

Ask God to show you how to live today.

"Lord, show me how to live my moments in ways that
glorify you and serve others. Walk with me today, my
Jesus. Amen."

Monday, December 24, 2018

Know that God is present with you and ready to converse.

"Thank you for being here with me again today. Let
me join the raining of praise upon you, Father, Son,
and Holy Spirit."

Read the gospel: Luke 1:67–79.

Then his father Zechariah was filled with the Holy
Spirit and spoke this prophecy:

> "Blessed be the Lord God of Israel,
>> for he has looked favorably on his people and
>> redeemed them.
> He has raised up a mighty savior for us
>> in the house of his servant David,
> as he spoke through the mouth of his holy proph-
>> ets from of old,
>> that we would be saved from our enemies and
>> from the hand of all who hate us.

Thus he has shown the mercy promised to our
ancestors,
and has remembered his holy covenant,
the oath that he swore to our ancestor Abraham,
to grant us that we, being rescued from the
hands of our enemies,
might serve him without fear, in holiness and
righteousness
before him all our days.
And you, child, will be called the prophet of the
Most High;
for you will go before the Lord to prepare his
ways,
to give knowledge of salvation to his people
by the forgiveness of their sins.
By the tender mercy of our God,
the dawn from on high will break upon us,
to give light to those who sit in darkness and in the
shadow of death,
to guide our feet into the way of peace."

Notice what you think and feel
as you read the gospel.

Zechariah, who doubted the angel's announcement
and was made mute for his unbelief, has seen the light,
and he uses his newly restored voice to proclaim the
greatness and mercy of God.

Pray as you are led for yourself and others.

"I cannot pray as beautifully as that, Lord, but I join my
heart with Zechariah's prayer. Thank you for lifting me
and giving me light. I pray for those in darkness . . ."
(Continue in your own words.)

Listen to Jesus.

God is the same today as he was when Zechariah prayed, for God is eternal. He dwells in light and holiness. Come to us, beloved. What else is Jesus saying to you?

Ask God to show you how to live today.

"Let my heart be stayed on you all the day long, Lord. Let me reflect upon your high and holy glory. Then I will seek you in humility and service. Amen."

THE CHRISTMAS SEASON
THROUGH EPIPHANY

In Christmas we can see how human history, that movement of the powerful of this world, is visited by the history of God. And God engages those who, confined to the margins of society, are the first beneficiaries of his gift, namely the salvation borne by Jesus. With the little ones and the scorned Jesus establishes a friendship that continues in time and that nourishes hope for a better future. . . . With them, in all ages, God wishes to build a new world, a world in which there are no longer rejected, mistreated and indigent people.

Pope Francis
December 27, 2017

Tuesday, December 25, 2018
The Nativity of the Lord

Know that God is present with you and ready to converse.

"Infant Jesus, I love you. You are God with us. Let me see you in your Word."

Read the gospel: John 1:1–18.

In the beginning was the Word, and the Word was with God, and the Word was God. He was in the beginning with God. All things came into being through him, and without him not one thing came into being. What has come into being in him was life, and the life was the light of all people. The light shines in the darkness, and the darkness did not overcome it.

There was a man sent from God, whose name was John. He came as a witness to testify to the light, so that all might believe through him. He himself was not the light, but he came to testify to the light. The true light, which enlightens everyone, was coming into the world.

He was in the world, and the world came into being through him; yet the world did not know him. He came to what was his own, and his own people did not accept him. But to all who received him, who believed in his name, he gave power to become children of God, who were born, not of blood or of the will of the flesh or of the will of man, but of God.

And the Word became flesh and lived among us, and we have seen his glory, the glory as of a father's only son, full of grace and truth. (John testified to him and cried out, "This was he of whom I said, 'He who comes after me ranks ahead of me because he was before me.'") From his fullness we have all received, grace upon grace. The law indeed was given through Moses; grace and truth came through Jesus Christ. No one has ever seen God. It is God the only Son, who is close to the Father's heart, who has made him known.

Notice what you think and feel as you read the gospel.

John the Evangelist emphasizes the cosmic meaning of the birth of Christ. Jesus, the Messiah, is eternal with God, the very Word of God, equal with God, the light against the darkness. Humans may choose the light if they are willing to abandon their sins and come to Christ for eternal life.

Pray as you are led for yourself and others.

"Glory and thanks to you, infant Savior. As I come to marvel at you today, I pray for all those in darkness. Let them come to your light . . ." (Continue in your own words.)

Listen to Jesus.

For love of all, I came to bring a blaze of light to the people of the world. Beloved disciple, you share God's mercy when you pray for those in darkness, for there are many who do not know me. What else is Jesus saying to you?

Ask God to show you how to live today.

"So I will continue to pray for those in darkness, Lord. Let me persevere in fervent prayer. Amen."

Wednesday, December 26, 2018

Know that God is present with you and ready to converse.

"Lord, I cling to you in good times and bad. Help me to persevere in faith and service by drawing strength from your Word."

Read the gospel: Matthew 10:17–22.

Jesus said, "Beware of them, for they will hand you over to councils and flog you in their synagogues; and you will be dragged before governors and kings because of me, as a testimony to them and the Gentiles. When they hand you over, do not worry about how you are to speak or what you are to say; for what you are to say will be given to you at that time; for it is not you who speak, but the Spirit of your Father speaking through you. Brother will betray brother to death, and a father his child, and children will rise against parents and have them put to death; and you will be hated by all because of my name. But the one who endures to the end will be saved."

Notice what you think and feel as you read the gospel.

Jesus speaks of the inevitability of rejection and persecution that comes from following him. He tells his disciples to trust God, for God is with them in these trials, and eternal reward will come.

Pray as you are led for yourself and others.

"Be with me when I experience persecution in any form. Lord, I pray for all those who are persecuted,

bullied, abused, or belittled for their faith in God . . ."
(Continue in your own words.)

Listen to Jesus.

God allows violence against his people, but justice will prevail. In me, your suffering will bear fruit unto eternal life. I have overcome the world. Child, apply yourself to doing good. What else is Jesus saying to you?

Ask God to show you how to live today.

"By your grace, Lord, I will persevere in doing good, even in the face of adversity, seeking peace, and working for justice for all. Amen."

Thursday, December 27, 2018

Know that God is present with you and ready to converse.

"Let me hear and believe your mighty Word, Lord."

Read the gospel: John 20:1a, 2–8.

Early on the first day of the week, while it was still dark, Mary Magdalene came to the tomb and saw that the stone had been removed from the tomb. . . . So she ran and went to Simon Peter and the other disciple, the one whom Jesus loved, and said to them, "They have taken the Lord out of the tomb, and we do not know where they have laid him." Then Peter and the other disciple set out and went towards the tomb. The two were running together, but the other disciple outran Peter and reached the tomb first. He bent down to look in and saw the linen wrappings lying there, but he did not go in. Then Simon Peter came, following him, and went into the tomb. He saw the linen wrappings lying there, and the cloth that had been on Jesus' head, not lying with the linen wrappings but rolled up in a place by itself. Then the other disciple, who reached the tomb first, also went in, and he saw and believed.

Notice what you think and feel as you read the gospel.

We see how the disciples react to Mary Magdalene's announcement of Jesus' empty tomb. They run to the tomb and see the grave, and immediately they believe Jesus has risen from the dead on the third day as he said he would. They would soon see the risen Lord with their own eyes.

Pray as you are led for yourself and others.

"Lord, I too believe you have risen; you abide forever with your Father in heaven in the unity of the Holy Spirit. But you continue your work among us, showing mercy and power on behalf of all, especially the poor and afflicted. Care for them, Lord . . ." (Continue in your own words.)

Listen to Jesus.

I do my work through my faithful servants, beloved. You believe and walk in my light. Trust me. Trust that I am working within you. What else is Jesus saying to you?

Ask God to show you how to live today.

"With you, Lord, I can do anything. I praise you for your mercy to all of us who need you. Amen."

Friday, December 28, 2018
Holy Innocents

Know that God is present with you and ready to converse.

"Lord, you work your will through triumphs and through tragedies. Teach me by your Word."

Read the gospel: Matthew 2:13–18.

An angel of the Lord appeared to Joseph in a dream and said, "Get up, take the child and his mother, and flee to Egypt, and remain there until I tell you; for Herod is about to search for the child, to destroy him." Then Joseph got up, took the child and his mother by night, and went to Egypt, and remained there until the death of Herod. This was to fulfill what had been spoken by the Lord through the prophet, "Out of Egypt I have called my son."

When Herod saw that he had been tricked by the wise men, he was infuriated, and he sent and killed all the children in and around Bethlehem who were two years old or under, according to the time that he had learned from the wise men. Then was fulfilled what had been spoken through the prophet Jeremiah.

Notice what you think and feel as you read the gospel.

While God guides the Holy Family to safety, he allows Herod to slaughter all the young children in and around Bethlehem. Why would he do such a thing? Matthew sees it as the fulfillment of a prophecy of Jeremiah, the Old Testament prophet (see Jer 31:15).

Pray as you are led for yourself and others.

"Let me trust you are also guiding me, Lord. Let me have compassion upon all who suffer, especially the children. Let your love execute justice and mercy, Lord . . ." (Continue in your own words.)

Listen to Jesus.

I do guide you, for you are a child in this holy family of believers. Have no fear of violence. God sees all and will mete out justice and reward. What else is Jesus saying to you?

Ask God to show you how to live today.

"I wish to grow in wisdom to understand the mysterious evil I see in the world. Give me great compassion for victims, Lord, and raise me up for your justice. Thank you. Amen."

Saturday, December 29, 2018

Know that God is present with you and ready to converse.

"Lord, the world long awaited you. Now that you have come, we rejoice. Let me understand your Word and obey it."

Read the gospel: Luke 2:22–35.

When the time came for their purification according to the law of Moses, they brought him up to Jerusalem to present him to the Lord (as it is written in the law of the Lord, "Every firstborn male shall be designated as holy to the Lord"), and they offered a sacrifice according to what is stated in the law of the Lord, "a pair of turtledoves or two young pigeons."

Now there was a man in Jerusalem whose name was Simeon; this man was righteous and devout, looking forward to the consolation of Israel, and the Holy Spirit rested on him. It had been revealed to him by the Holy Spirit that he would not see death before he had seen the Lord's Messiah. Guided by the Spirit, Simeon came into the temple; and when the parents brought in the child Jesus, to do for him what was customary under the law, Simeon took him in his arms and praised God, saying,

> "Master, now you are dismissing your servant in peace,
>   according to your word;
> for my eyes have seen your salvation,
>   which you have prepared in the presence of all peoples,
> a light for revelation to the Gentiles
>   and for glory to your people Israel."

And the child's father and mother were amazed at what was being said about him. Then Simeon blessed them and said to his mother Mary, "This child is destined for the falling and the rising of many in Israel, and to be a sign that will be opposed so that the inner thoughts of many will be revealed—and a sword will pierce your own soul too."

Notice what you think and feel as you read the gospel.

When Jesus is only a few weeks old, can barely lift his own head up, and is still completely dependent on his human parents for survival, they present him at the Temple. Simeon recognizes in this helpless infant the salvation of the entire world.

Pray as you are led for yourself and others.

"Lord, may I too recognize you as I walk through life, and at the end of my life may I give you thanks that I have known you. I pray for those who do not know you . . ." (Continue in your own words.)

Listen to Jesus.

Recognize me in others, my dear one. See me in the faces of children, the poor, the hungry, the sick, the homeless, the imprisoned, the persecuted, and the dying. What else is Jesus saying to you?

Ask God to show you how to live today.

"Only by your grace do I have the power to obey you in this. Yet I resolve to do it. Show me how to obey today. I will trust you for grace. Thank you. Make me more and more a temple of your Spirit. Amen."

Sunday, December 30, 2018
Holy Family

**Know that God is present with
you and ready to converse.**

"Wise Child, I turn to your Word for your Wisdom."

Read the gospel: Luke 2:41–52.

Now every year his parents went to Jerusalem for the festival of the Passover. And when he was twelve years old, they went up as usual for the festival. When the festival was ended and they started to return, the boy Jesus stayed behind in Jerusalem, but his parents did not know it. Assuming that he was in the group of travelers, they went a day's journey. Then they started to look for him among their relatives and friends. When they did not find him, they returned to Jerusalem to search for him. After three days they found him in the temple, sitting among the teachers, listening to them and asking them questions. And all who heard him were amazed at his understanding and his answers. When his parents saw him they were astonished; and his mother said to him, "Child, why have you treated us like this? Look, your father and I have been searching for you in great anxiety." He said to them, "Why were you searching for me? Did you not know that I must be in my Father's house?" But they did not understand what he said to them. Then he went down with them and came to Nazareth, and was obedient to them. His mother treasured all these things in her heart.

And Jesus increased in wisdom and in years, and in divine and human favor.

Notice what you think and feel as you read the gospel.

Mary is hurt by the actions of her adolescent son and confused by his words; she does not fully understand, but she treasures the experiences and the memories.

Pray as you are led for yourself and others.

"As I experience you in my life, Lord, let me build up grateful memories of our time together. Those memories will strengthen my faith and joy to the end of my life . . ." (Continue in your own words.)

Listen to Jesus.

I am with you now and to the end, beloved. Ask me for whatever you want today. What else is Jesus saying to you?

Ask God to show you how to live today.

"Help me stay very close to you every moment of this day. Let me share our moments with others. Amen."

Monday, December 31, 2018

**Know that God is present with
you and ready to converse.**

"You are with me now, mighty Jesus. Let me know you in your Word."

Read the gospel: John 1:1–18.

In the beginning was the Word, and the Word was with God, and the Word was God. He was in the beginning with God. All things came into being through him, and without him not one thing came into being. What has come into being in him was life, and the life was the light of all people. The light shines in the darkness, and the darkness did not overcome it.

There was a man sent from God, whose name was John. He came as a witness to testify to the light, so that all might believe through him. He himself was not the light, but he came to testify to the light. The true light, which enlightens everyone, was coming into the world.

He was in the world, and the world came into being through him; yet the world did not know him. He came to what was his own, and his own people did not accept him. But to all who received him, who believed in his name, he gave power to become children of God, who were born, not of blood or of the will of the flesh or of the will of man, but of God.

And the Word became flesh and lived among us, and we have seen his glory, the glory as of a father's only son, full of grace and truth. (John testified to him and cried out, "This was he of whom I said, 'He who comes after me ranks ahead of me because he was before me.'") From his fullness we have all received, grace upon grace. The law indeed was given through Moses; grace and truth came through Jesus Christ. No one has ever seen God. It is God the only Son, who is close to the Father's heart, who has made him known.

Notice what you think and feel as you read the gospel.

John begins his gospel with this profound description of the Christ, eternal with God yet born in time on earth to bring to all peoples the revelation of the Almighty God of infinite love and mercy. Who can take it in? But this is not just a description. It is a call to open our eyes to the Light of God, to accept God's everlasting Life.

Pray as you are led for yourself and others.

"God, I do not want to miss my moment to know you and love you as you are. Make me truly a child of God and let multitudes come to you . . ." (Continue in your own words.)

Listen to Jesus.

I rejoice in your love, child of God. I hear your prayer and continue to pour out my mercy upon people—more than you can know. I work in a person's heart and soul. What else is Jesus saying to you?

Ask God to show you how to live today.

"You are good to me, Lord. Show me how to be good to others today. Glory to God in the highest. Amen."

THE POPE'S MONTHLY PRAYER INTENTION FOR JANUARY 2019

That young people, especially in Latin America, follow the example of Mary and respond to the call of the Lord to communicate the joy of the Gospel to the world.

Tuesday, January 1, 2019
Blessed Virgin Mary, Mother of God

Know that God is present with you and ready to converse.
"Humble, holy infant, I come with the shepherds in wonder to adore you."

Read the gospel: Luke 2:16–21.
So the shepherds went with haste and found Mary and Joseph, and the child lying in the manger. When they saw this, they made known what had been told them about this child; and all who heard it were amazed at what the shepherds told them. But Mary treasured all these words and pondered them in her heart. The shepherds returned, glorifying and praising God for all they had heard and seen, as it had been told them.

After eight days had passed, it was time to circumcise the child; and he was called Jesus, the name given by the angel before he was conceived in the womb.

Notice what you think and feel as you read the gospel.

The shepherds saw the heavenly host praising God and were directed to the stable by an angel. They find Mary, Joseph, and the infant in the manger. Mary treasures the words of the shepherds and ponders them in her heart. What shall this child become? The shepherds return to their fields, rejoicing in God.

Pray as you are led for yourself and others.

"I praise the works of God in history and in my life. Let God's words and works continue to advance the kingdom. I think of these needs . . ." (Continue in your own words.)

Listen to Jesus.

Dear one, beginning with my birth, I have revealed to humankind the goodness and the glory of God, the Almighty, who offers eternal life to all. Do not despair. I am with you, and God is God. What else is Jesus saying to you?

Ask God to show you how to live today.

"Let me, like the shepherds, come and worship and be near you and then carry your presence with me to proclaim you to the world. Amen."

Wednesday, January 2, 2019

Know that God is present with you and ready to converse.

"You are with me now, Lord. Let me know you in your Word."

Read the gospel: John 1:19–28.

This is the testimony given by John when the Jews sent priests and Levites from Jerusalem to ask him, "Who are you?" He confessed and did not deny it, but confessed, "I am not the Messiah." And they asked him, "What then? Are you Elijah?" He said, "I am not." "Are you the prophet?" He answered, "No." Then they said to him, "Who are you? Let us have an answer for those who sent us. What do you say about yourself?" He said,

> "I am the voice of one crying out in the wilderness, 'Make straight the way of the Lord,'"

as the prophet Isaiah said.

Now they had been sent from the Pharisees. They asked him, "Why then are you baptizing if you are neither the Messiah, nor Elijah, nor the prophet?" John answered them, "I baptize with water. Among you stands one whom you do not know, the one who is coming after me; I am not worthy to untie the thong of his sandal." This took place in Bethany across the Jordan where John was baptizing.

Notice what you think and feel as you read the gospel.

John the Baptist is interrogated by the priests and Levites. They are probably worried about the many people who have flocked to his preaching and baptisms. Who is he? He answers with scripture from Isaiah that he is the voice crying in the wilderness to make straight the way of the Lord. He goes on to tell them to expect one greater, even now standing among them. One supposes they were not pleased by his answers.

Pray as you are led for yourself and others.

"God, I look to you this moment. Baptize me with your Spirit that I may love and serve you better, especially in these areas . . ." (Continue in your own words.)

Listen to Jesus.

Child of God, follow me and all will be well with you. I rejoice in your love. What else is Jesus saying to you?

Ask God to show you how to live today.

"How can I straighten the way for you today, Lord? Show me the right path, and use me to fix what is crooked and bent. Amen."

Thursday, January 3, 2019

Know that God is present with you and ready to converse.

"Let me believe and receive the words of your prophets, Lord, for they speak what they know."

Read the gospel: John 1:29–34.

The next day John saw Jesus coming towards him and declared, "Here is the Lamb of God who takes away the sin of the world! This is he of whom I said, 'After me comes a man who ranks ahead of me because he was before me.' I myself did not know him; but I came baptizing with water for this reason, that he might be revealed to Israel." And John testified, "I saw the Spirit descending from heaven like a dove, and it remained on him. I myself did not know him, but the one who sent me to baptize with water said to me, 'He on whom you see the Spirit descend and remain is the one who baptizes with the Holy Spirit.' And I myself have seen and have testified that this is the Son of God."

Notice what you think and feel as you read the gospel.

John recognizes Jesus as the Lamb of God who takes away the sin of the world. He has prophetic knowledge from God that Jesus is destined to be the sacrificial Lamb of God. He certainly knows Jesus ranks ahead of him and existed before him. He testifies that Jesus is the Son of God, because he saw the Spirit descend and remain on him.

Pray as you are led for yourself and others.

"Lamb of God, take away my sins. Fill me with your Holy Spirit, that I may proclaim you . . ." (Continue in your own words.)

Listen to Jesus.

Seek me in the sacraments, dear disciple, and the Spirit will shower you with gifts, and you will bear fruit, giving my gifts to others. What else is Jesus saying to you?

Ask God to show you how to live today.

"Guide me in my giving, doing, and praying today, Lord. Let me give as generously as I have received. Thank you for taking away my sins, Lamb of God. Amen."

Friday, January 4, 2019

Know that God is present with you and ready to converse.

"You have come, Lord. Let me find and love the Lamb of God."

Read the gospel: John 1:35–42.

The next day John again was standing with two of his disciples, and as he watched Jesus walk by, he exclaimed, "Look, here is the Lamb of God!" The two disciples heard him say this, and they followed Jesus. When Jesus turned and saw them following, he said to them, "What are you looking for?" They said to him, "Rabbi" (which translated means Teacher), "where are you staying?" He said to them, "Come and see." They came and saw where he was staying, and they remained with him that day. It was about four o'clock in the afternoon. One of the two who heard John speak and followed him was Andrew, Simon Peter's brother. He first found his brother Simon and said to him, "We have found the Messiah" (which is translated Anointed). He brought Simon to Jesus, who looked at him and said, "You are Simon son of John. You are to be called Cephas" (which is translated Peter).

Notice what you think and feel as you read the gospel.

Jesus' first disciples are drawn to him by the words of John the Baptist. Jesus does not recruit them but invites them to come and see.

Pray as you are led for yourself and others.

"Lord, let me come and see you. Please know me as your own and let me be a true disciple that others may also come to you . . ." (Continue in your own words.)

Listen to Jesus.

Come, follow me, forsaking all. Set your heart and mind on the will of God. God will guide you and you will overcome the world and receive eternal life. What else is Jesus saying to you?

Ask God to show you how to live today.

"Only by your grace can I follow you purely and truly, Lord. Fill me and make me new. Amen."

Saturday, January 5, 2019

Know that God is present with you and ready to converse.

"You are present, Lord. Call me to yourself by your Word."

Read the gospel: John 1:43–51.

The next day Jesus decided to go to Galilee. He found Philip and said to him, "Follow me." Now Philip was from Bethsaida, the city of Andrew and Peter. Philip found Nathanael and said to him, "We have found him about whom Moses in the law and also the prophets wrote, Jesus son of Joseph from Nazareth." Nathanael said to him, "Can anything good come out of Nazareth?" Philip said to him, "Come and see." When Jesus saw Nathanael coming towards him, he said of him, "Here is truly an Israelite in whom there is no deceit!" Nathanael asked him, "Where did you come to know me?" Jesus answered, "I saw you under the fig tree before Philip called you." Nathanael replied, "Rabbi, you are the Son of God! You are the King of Israel!" Jesus answered, "Do you believe because I told you that I saw you under the fig tree? You will see greater things than these." And he said to him, "Very truly, I tell you, you will see heaven opened and the angels of God ascending and descending upon the Son of Man."

Notice what you think and feel as you read the gospel.

Why is it amazing to Nathanael that Jesus saw him under the fig tree? Yet Jesus didn't just notice him in passing. Jesus saw him, saw his character and his honesty; and Nathanael, in turn, sees something about who Jesus is: the Son of God and the King of Israel.

Pray as you are led for yourself and others.

"Lord, give me the vision to see you and, seeing, to follow you, and let me share your truth with all whom I encounter . . ." (Continue in your own words.)

Listen to Jesus.

Beloved disciple, I see you. Follow me closely and you will be part of the great work of God, the salvation of the world. What else is Jesus saying to you?

Ask God to show you how to live today.

"Open my eyes to your will for me, Lord, especially the knowledge of what to do in situations and opportunities I might miss. Thank you. Amen."

Sunday, January 6, 2019
Epiphany of the Lord

Know that God is present with you and ready to converse.

"Lord, you are Father of the Word, your beloved Son. Let me also adore him by meditating on your Word."

Read the gospel: Matthew 2:1–12.

In the time of King Herod, after Jesus was born in Bethlehem of Judea, wise men from the East came to Jerusalem, asking, "Where is the child who has been born king of the Jews? For we observed his star at its rising, and have come to pay him homage." When King Herod heard this, he was frightened, and all Jerusalem with him; and calling together all the chief priests and scribes of the people, he inquired of them where the Messiah was to be born. They told him, "In Bethlehem of Judea; for so it has been written by the prophet:

'And you, Bethlehem, in the land of Judah,
    are by no means least among the rulers of
        Judah;
for from you shall come a ruler
    who is to shepherd my people Israel.'"

Then Herod secretly called for the wise men and learned from them the exact time when the star had appeared. Then he sent them to Bethlehem, saying, "Go and search diligently for the child; and when you have found him, bring me word so that I may also go and pay him homage." When they had heard the king, they set out; and there, ahead of them, went the star that they had seen at its rising, until it stopped over the place where the child was. When they saw that the star had stopped, they were overwhelmed with joy. On entering the house, they saw the child with Mary his mother; and they knelt down and paid him homage. Then, opening their treasure-chests, they offered him gifts of gold, frankincense, and myrrh. And having been warned in a dream not to return to Herod, they left for their own country by another road.

Notice what you think and feel as you read the gospel.

Good and evil operate together in this gospel, as the wise men come to pay homage to the infant King and Herod plots to thwart this threat to his power. The kings kneel before the child and give him their precious gifts. Wisely, they do not return to Herod but return home by another road.

Pray as you are led for yourself and others.

"Lord, you have come for all people, any who will say yes to you. Please give all people the chance to receive you . . ." (Continue in your own words.)

Listen to Jesus.

I love your heart for others, my beloved. God is mercy and understands the prison of sin in which the world is locked. But by power he will restore righteousness and peace forever. Trust in God. What else is Jesus saying to you?

Ask God to show you how to live today.

"I want to be part of God's work, Jesus, walking more closely with you. How may I please you today? Amen."

Monday, January 7, 2019

Know that God is present with you and ready to converse.

"Lord, reveal your glory to me. I turn to your Word for light and life." God Nature love, life and night

Read the gospel: Matthew 4:12–17.

Now when Jesus heard that John had been arrested, he withdrew to Galilee. He left Nazareth and made his home in Capernaum by the lake, in the territory of Zebulun and Naphtali, so that what had been spoken through the prophet Isaiah might be fulfilled:

> "Land of Zebulun, land of Naphtali,
>   on the road by the sea, across the Jordan, Gal-
>   ilee of the Gentiles—
> the people who sat in darkness
>   have seen a great light,
> and for those who sat in the region and shadow
>   of death
>   light has dawned."

From that time Jesus began to proclaim, "Repent, for the kingdom of heaven has come near."

Notice what you think and feel as you read the gospel.

Jesus moves from Nazareth to Capernaum to begin his ministry, preaching repentance. He is the light that has come into the land of darkness. He is the Light of the World.

Pray as you are led for yourself and others.

"Shine your light on me, Redeemer, for I am a sinner. Let my greatest longing be to enter the kingdom of heaven so that I may love and praise you forever . . ." (Continue in your own words.)

Listen to Jesus.

Open yourself to me, beloved, and I will fill you with light and dispel all your darkness. What else is Jesus saying to you?

Ask God to show you how to live today.

"I worship you and will walk in the light of your presence today. Let me do something to help someone in need. Amen."

Tuesday, January 8, 2019

Know that God is present with you and ready to converse.

"Bread of Life, Word of God, let me know you in your Word."

Read the gospel: Mark 6:34–44.

As Jesus went ashore, he saw a great crowd; and he had compassion for them, because they were like sheep without a shepherd; and he began to teach them many things. When it grew late, his disciples came to him and said, "This is a deserted place, and the hour is now very late; send them away so that they may go into the surrounding country and villages and buy something for themselves to eat." But he answered them, "You give them something to eat." They said to him, "Are we to go and buy two hundred denarii worth of bread, and give it to them to eat?" And he said to them, "How many loaves have you? Go and see." When they had found out, they said, "Five, and two fish." Then he ordered them to get all the people to sit down in groups on the green grass. So they sat down in groups of hundreds and of fifties. Taking the five loaves and the two fish, he looked up to heaven, and blessed and broke the loaves, and gave them to his disciples to set before the people; and he divided the two fish among them all. And all ate and were filled; and they took up twelve baskets full of broken pieces and of the fish. Those who had eaten the loaves numbered five thousand men.

Notice what you think and feel as you read the gospel.

Jesus feeds a crowd of five thousand with five loaves and two fish, with twelve basketfuls remaining. Out of compassion, he shows his power to provide for the people's need.

Pray as you are led for yourself and others.

"Jesus, I have needs too. Help me to trust you to provide for me. I think of others who also have needs. Feed them, Lord . . ." (Continue in your own words.)

Listen to Jesus.

I came to the world because of the love of my Father. So I come to you today. You have entrusted yourself to me, beloved, and I am trustworthy. What else is Jesus saying to you?

Ask God to show you how to live today.

"Lord, please call others into this wonderful friendship with you. Open the eyes and hearts of those who are closed to you. Let me know what I may do to help. Amen."

Wednesday, January 9, 2019

Know that God is present with you and ready to converse.

"Jesus, break up the hardness of my heart that I may trust in you by the power of your Word."

Read the gospel: Mark 6:45–52.

Immediately Jesus made his disciples get into the boat and go on ahead to the other side, to Bethsaida, while he dismissed the crowd. After saying farewell to them, he went up on the mountain to pray.

When evening came, the boat was out on the lake, and he was alone on the land. When he saw that they were straining at the oars against an adverse wind, he came towards them early in the morning, walking on the lake. He intended to pass them by. But when they saw him walking on the lake, they thought it was a ghost and cried out; for they all saw him and were terrified. But immediately he spoke to them and said, "Take heart, it is I; do not be afraid." Then he got into the boat with them and the wind ceased. And they were utterly astounded, for they did not understand about the loaves, but their hearts were hardened.

Notice what you think and feel as you read the gospel.

The disciples barely have time to accept the miracle that Jesus has performed before he sends them off in the boat. "Who is this man?" they must have asked themselves. "What did he just do?" And here he comes, walking toward them on the surface of the water, and then his presence calms the wind they've been fighting all evening. "Who is this man?" Until they can answer that question, they will be afraid.

Pray as you are led for yourself and others.

"Let your love cast out all fear in me, dear Jesus. Let your love soften my heart in love for others . . ." (Continue in your own words.)

Listen to Jesus.

As you come to know me better, dear disciple, you will lose your fears more and more. You will understand how trustworthy I am. You will be an example to others. What else is Jesus saying to you?

Ask God to show you how to live today.

"Let me hear your voice of consolation and reassurance all day long, Lord. Let me reflect to others your peace and love. Amen."

Thursday, January 10, 2019

Know that God is present with you and ready to converse.

"You are with me, Lord. Let me hear your Good News."

Read the gospel: Luke 4:14–22.

Then Jesus, filled with the power of the Spirit, returned to Galilee, and a report about him spread through all the surrounding country. He began to teach in their synagogues and was praised by everyone.

When he came to Nazareth, where he had been brought up, he went to the synagogue on the sabbath day, as was his custom. He stood up to read, and the scroll of the prophet Isaiah was given to him. He unrolled the scroll and found the place where it was written:

> "The Spirit of the Lord is upon me,
>> because he has anointed me
>>> to bring good news to the poor.
> He has sent me to proclaim release to the captives
>> and recovery of sight to the blind,
>>> to let the oppressed go free,
> to proclaim the year of the Lord's favor."

And he rolled up the scroll, gave it back to the attendant, and sat down. The eyes of all in the synagogue were fixed on him. Then he began to say to them, "Today this scripture has been fulfilled in your hearing." All spoke well of him and were amazed at the gracious words that came from his mouth. They said, "Is not this Joseph's son?"

Notice what you think and feel as you read the gospel.

Jesus returns to Nazareth and preaches in his home synagogue to people who have known him all his life. They are amazed and say, "Is not this Joseph's son?" Clearly, they are puzzled too.

Pray as you are led for yourself and others.

"Lord, let me not doubt you. Keep my faith fresh and alive. Let me serve all those you have given me . . ." (Continue in your own words.)

Listen to Jesus.

I will continue to teach you as you listen to me and the Word of God. Follow me. What else is Jesus saying to you?

Ask God to show you how to live today.

"Amid doubts and confusions, Lord, I resolve to follow you faithfully today. I glorify you, Teacher. Amen."

Friday, January 11, 2019

Know that God is present with you and ready to converse.

"Jesus, you have power to heal. Help me to come to you for complete healing through the power of your Word."

Read the gospel: Luke 5:12–16.

Once, when Jesus was in one of the cities, there was a man covered with leprosy. When he saw Jesus, he bowed with his face to the ground and begged him, "Lord, if you choose, you can make me clean." Then Jesus stretched out his hand, touched him, and said, "I do choose. Be made clean." Immediately the leprosy left him. And he ordered him to tell no one. "Go," he said, "and show yourself to the priest, and, as Moses commanded, make an offering for your cleansing, for a testimony to them." But now more than ever the word about Jesus spread abroad; many crowds would gather to hear him and to be cured of their diseases. But he would withdraw to deserted places and pray.

Notice what you think and feel as you read the gospel.

The leper seems to doubt whether Jesus will want to heal him, but Jesus reassures him and heals him of his disease. Jesus tells him to tell no one but the priest and to make the prescribed offering. Yet the news about Jesus spread rapidly, so Jesus withdraws to pray.

Pray as you are led for yourself and others.

"Jesus, what is my critical disease? Do you choose to heal me? Show me and heal me. I pray for those who suffer as I do . . ." (Continue in your own words.)

Listen to Jesus.

I do choose to heal you, child. Pray boldly for what you need. I will answer your prayers for yourself and for others. What else is Jesus saying to you?

Ask God to show you how to live today.

"I will obey, Lord, giving thanks to you and offering myself for the good of others. Amen."

Saturday, January 12, 2019

Know that God is present with you and ready to converse.

"Lord, it is common for your people to dispute the truth and the right way. Let me find simple truth in your Word and adhere to it."

Read the gospel: John 3:22–30.

After this Jesus and his disciples went into the Judean countryside, and he spent some time there with them and baptized. John also was baptizing at Aenon near

Salim because water was abundant there; and people kept coming and were being baptized—John, of course, had not yet been thrown into prison.

Now a discussion about purification arose between John's disciples and a Jew. They came to John and said to him, "Rabbi, the one who was with you across the Jordan, to whom you testified, here he is baptizing, and all are going to him." John answered, "No one can receive anything except what has been given from heaven. You yourselves are my witnesses that I said, 'I am not the Messiah, but I have been sent ahead of him.' He who has the bride is the bridegroom. The friend of the bridegroom, who stands and hears him, rejoices greatly at the bridegroom's voice. For this reason my joy has been fulfilled. He must increase, but I must decrease."

Notice what you think and feel as you read the gospel.

John's disciples are challenged by Jesus' preaching and baptisms. Who should they follow? John tells them he is not the Messiah but the one who goes before the Messiah, not the bridegroom but the friend of the bridegroom.

Pray as you are led for yourself and others.

"Lord, I thank you for John the Baptist. Give me that kind of humility, honesty, and courage in my life . . ." (Continue in your own words.)

Listen to Jesus.

You are right to honor John. You do not err in wanting his virtues. Seek to practice them. I am with you. What else is Jesus saying to you?

Ask God to show you how to live today.

"Thank you for the privilege of following you. Lead me forward and help me serve those in need. Amen."

Sunday, January 13, 2019
Baptism of the Lord

Know that God is present with you and ready to converse.

"I come into your presence, Lord. Renew my baptism by your Word."

Read the gospel: Luke 3:15–16, 21–22.

As the people were filled with expectation, and all were questioning in their hearts concerning John, whether he might be the Messiah, John answered all of them by saying, "I baptize you with water; but one who is more powerful than I is coming; I am not worthy to untie the thong of his sandals. He will baptize you with the Holy Spirit and fire." . . .

Now when all the people were baptized, and when Jesus also had been baptized and was praying, the heaven was opened, and the Holy Spirit descended upon him in bodily form like a dove. And a voice came from heaven, "You are my Son, the Beloved; with you I am well pleased."

Notice what you think and feel as you read the gospel.

Water washes, but fire purifies. John's baptism washes away sins; Jesus burns them to ash in the fire of his love, which is the Holy Spirit.

Pray as you are led for yourself and others.
"I long for the fire of your Holy Spirit, Lord. Let it renew me and renew all the earth . . ." (Continue in your own words.)

Listen to Jesus.
I give you my Spirit, beloved. In you I am well pleased for you have set your heart upon me. Walk in faith, hope, and love. Follow me. What else is Jesus saying to you?

Ask God to show you how to live today.
"By the power of your Spirit, Lord, let me live my life glorifying you. Amen."

The Pope's Worldwide Prayer Network is an international ecclesial ministry served by the Jesuits that reaches more than 50 million participants worldwide through its popular website, talks, conferences, radio outreach, publications, and retreats. Each year the Holy Father asks that Christians and non-Christians alike join in praying for his particular intentions on the challenges facing humanity. The regional US–Canadian office can be found at popesprayerusa.net and popesprayercanada.net.